THIS NOTEBOOK BELONGS TO ....

CONTACT ....

See our range of fine, illustrated books, ebooks, notebooks and art calendars:
www.flametreepublishing.com

This is a **FLAME TREE NOTEBOOK**
Published and © copyright 2019 Flame Tree Publishing Ltd

FTNB222 • 978-1-78755-559-4

Cover image based on a detail from
Study for *Documents Décoratifs*, Plate 12
by Alphonse Mucha (1860–1939)
Produced by Flame Tree Publishing under license granted by Mucha Ltd
© Mucha Trust 2019, www.muchafoundation.org

Alphonse Mucha was a defining figure of the Art Nouveau era and is beloved for his enchanting,
highly-stylized illustrations. This charming study was created for his style book, *Documents
Décoratifs*, published by the Librarie Centrale des Beaux-Arts, Paris, in 1901. This portfolio
of Mucha's work was published at height of his popularity, and would go on to influence
the legions of artists and designers seeking to emulate 'Le Style Mucha'.

FLAME TREE PUBLISHING | The Art of Fine Gifts
6 Melbray Mews, London SW6 3NS, United Kingdom